Observing the Invisible

ALSO BY KELLY CHERRY

POETRY
Beholder's Eye
Quartet for J. Robert Oppenheimer
The Life and Death of Poetry
The Retreats of Thought
Hazard and Prospect: New and
　Selected Poems
Rising Venus
Death and Transfiguration
God's Loud Hand
Natural Theology
Relativity: A Point of View
Lovers and Agnostics

FICTION
Temporium
Twelve Women in a Country
　Called America
A Kind of Dream
The Woman Who
We Can Still Be Friends
The Society of Friends
My Life and Dr. Joyce Brothers
The Lost Traveller's Dream
In the Wink of an Eye
Augusta Played
Sick and Full of Burning

NONFICTION
Girl in a Library: On Women
　Writers and the Writing Life
History, Passion, Freedom, Death,
　and Hope: Prose about Poetry
Writing the World
The Exiled Heart: A Meditative
　Autobiography

CHAPBOOKS & LIMITED EDITIONS
Weather
Physics for Poets (poems)
Vectors: J. Robert Oppenheimer:
　The Years before the Bomb (poems)
The Globe and the Brain (essay)
Welsh Table Talk (poems)
An Other Woman (poem)
The Poem (essay)
Time out of Mind (poems)
Benjamin John (poem)
Songs for a Soviet Composer (poems)
Conversion (story)

OTHER
A Kelly Cherry Reader (stories,
　novel excerpts, essay,
　memoir, eight poems)

TRANSLATIONS
"Antigone," in *Sophocles, 2*
"Octavia," in *Seneca: The Tragedies,
　Volume II*

KELLY CHERRY

Observing the Invisible

POEMS

Louisiana State University Press | Baton Rouge

Published by Louisiana State University Press
Copyright © 2019 by Kelly Cherry
All rights reserved
Manufactured in the United States of America
LSU Press Paperback Original
First printing

DESIGNER: *Mandy McDonald Scallan*
TYPEFACE: *Whitman*
PRINTER AND BINDER: *LSI*

Cataloging-in-Publication Data are available from the Library of Congress.

ISBN 978-0-8071-7007-6 (pbk.: alk. paper) — ISBN 978-0-8071-7183-7 (pdf) — ISBN 978-0-8071-7184-4 (epub)

The paper in this book meets the guidelines for permanence and durability of the Committee on Production Guidelines for Book Longevity of the Council on Library Resources.♾

Vision is the art of seeing things invisible.
—JONATHAN SWIFT
Thoughts on Various Subjects from Miscellanies

We are more closely connected to the invisible than to the visible.
—NOVALIS
Das Allgemeine Brouillon, §251

... we look not at the things which are seen, but at the things which are not seen: for the things which are seen are temporal; but the things which are not seen are eternal.
—II COR., KJV

Power, time, gravity, love. The forces that really kick ass are all invisible.
—DAVID MITCHELL
Cloud Atlas

Contents

I

Alice These Days 3
This Universal Contraption 4
Alpha and Omega 5
Musica Universalis 6
Music and Mathematics 7
Fantastic the Distances 8
Of Stars 9
SETI 10
The Horsehead Nebula 11
Bipolar Nebulae 12
Andromeda 13
A Dialogue between Mars and Venus 15
The World as Hologram 16
Blowback 17
Occam's Razor 18
Astronomer and Telescope 19
Everything Lifted Off from the Earth 21

II

Cogitation 25

Memories 26

Riga 1975 27

Reverie 28

Imagination 29

In an Alternate World 30

Seemingly Enigmatic 31

On the Perception of Time 32

Patterning 33

The Nature of Hypothesis 35

Metaphor as Method 36

On Intuition 37

Invention 38

On Mathematical Logic 39

Consilience 40

Contemplation as Complication 41

Fog at Emerald Island, North Carolina 42

III

We Pray for These and All 45

Absence 46

Small Errors with Gigantic Consequences 47

The Dog of Brownian Motion 48

Quanta 49

Atomism 50

The God Particle 51

Heaven on Earth 53

Demodex Folliculorum 54
Regarding Clouds 55
In the Desert 56
The Wind 57
DNA 58
Negative Numbers 60
Radiation 61
Light 63
Dark Energy 64

IV

Childhood and God 67
Conscience 68
Complicity 69
Snow in Southwest Minnesota 70
The Visitors 71
Their Pleas 72
They Are More Present 73
Looking for My Dead Mother's Phone Number 74
An Apology 75
The Cliffs of Nothingness 76
Of Love and Time 78
The Loneliness of the Human Being 79
Geophysics 80
The Studio 82
The Right Words 83

Acknowledgments 85

Alice These Days

A universe of pulsars and dark matter,
of stars spectacular with raging fire,
of ringed or cloudy worlds a mad hatter
might find bizarre, something like a choir
of mutes, deaf mutes, who nevertheless inspire
a sound so beautiful it grips the heart
and moves the mind in a twisting, turning gyre
no Yeats could make conform to credible art.

What is this wonderland in which we live,
this physics that seems magical as alchemy,
incomprehensible except to those
who know the formulas, equations, laws
and quantum contradictions, the dark energy
we cannot see or feel but must believe?

This Universal Contraption

Let's think about this universal contraption
of wheels, rings, shooting stars, comets,
red giants and white dwarves, and the persistent note
of B-flat that issues from a black hole
in the Perseus Galaxy and is fifty-seven
reverberant octaves below middle C
(the limited human ear cannot hear it).
A Rube Goldberg creation, made mostly
of dark matter and dark energy,
neither of which can the human eye see.
Other senses? Our noses are pretty much useless,
as any dog can tell you. Taste? To lick
or not to lick: that is the question and
it is an easy one to answer. Therefore,
what can touch teach us about the whole
kit and caboodle? The scientists say that dark
energy is in us, moves right through us, flesh
and bone and blood, as we through it and yet
and probably forever feel it not.
I like to think that after we die and return
to stardust (whence we came), we'll shrug off the weight
of light years, slide steel blades on our shoes,
and lean headfirst into space-time, our faces
braving the cold solar air as we skate
the sideways crazy 8 of infinity.

Alpha and Omega

A point of tension, an inflection point—
"without dimension" being the definition
of a point (and out of time, given that
Einstein proved that time cannot exist
without space)—an inflection point, then, that bursts
into being, ex nihilo, a massless light
that transgresses the nothing before to make
a universe, space expanding, as
an unknown dark something enters the unseen
picture. And now the firmament's swirling gases
gather themselves into contained wildfires.
Fragments chill, clusters becoming planets
or moons or meteors or belts of roving
asteroids. The curvature of space
is key, accounting for gravity.
The universe is in no hurry; it has
all the time in the world. And so time
passes, at very much a leisurely pace,
and yet the universe, which is expanding,
expands at an accelerating speed
and will continue to expand, becoming
thin and shredded as bank statements run
through a paper shredder. Or say thin and shredded
as tissue used to staunch a child's hot tears.
Or might a cycle be continued and
another universe begun? Or do
other universes already exist
in the loose threads of this one? And do the Fates
spin, measure, and snip methodically?
Then why are they cackling, hags with toothless gums?

Why are they throwing dice against a wall?

Musica Universalis

The classical harmony of the spheres
abrades any doubt about
the message of the music: that
he who hears must write it down
for humankind or for that one soul
who happens on the long-lost score
wherein the wheeling cosmos serenades
the brilliance of its stars,
the mystery at its core.

Music and Mathematics

A mathematical proof is like a star,
a thing whose own combustible energy
induces it to shine more brightly than air.
A tautness in the reasoning will give rise
to music, of the most celestial sort,
with which clarity cannot fail to keep company.
The dreaminess that touches the faces of thinkers
deserves to be taken as a sign of benediction,
for who's more blessed than one who hears the music
of heavenly spheres? It settles in the ears,
audible logic, singing, shining numbers
keyed to eternity, Platonic proof
that we can know that which we know not.

Fantastic the Distances

Fantastic the distances, the temperatures,
the bending light that bears time on its back,
freight shipped from the first minimicroinstant

to our otherwise overlookable planet on
the spiral arm of an average galaxy on
the fringy outskirts of almost everything.

Now it's here—light that lets us see,
that lets us be seen, that celebrates existence,
that elates our miserable collapsed souls,

though how much of *it* do we see? A prismatic
spectrum stretching from red to deep violet.
Yet it embraces every tint and hue,

a blue as bright as the bright blue that blinded
Lazarus emerging from his tomb, a purple
pillowy enough to suffocate a man,

a white composed of all the colors and purer
than guardian angels, who willfully tarnish their wings
dallying in earth's stony valley of death.

Of Stars

As if a Johnny Appleseed flung far
and wide across the universe bounty
beyond belief, munificent and free,
of stars of every magnitude that bloom
hot red or fervent orange in galaxies
beyond our aided, telescopic sight,
the stars we see are but a promise, a
preview, of the unaccountably generous—
say: staggering—number of stars there actually are.

As if the wanderer had sowed, by dark,
huge handfuls of seeds, largesse of what will ripen.

SETI

Radio telescopes like massive elephant ears,
pricked to catch the least word or code
whispered across the universe, eavesdropping
on the steady murmur of deep space, muffled
as if underwater. Do we hear the clash
of civilizations, formerly great nations
battling others for land, water, oil?
Oh wait—that's Earth. Surely in outer space
we'll find a species superior to our own.
Surely such beings are even now texting
urgent messages to us: *We want
nothing to do with you. Humans, stay home.*

The Horsehead Nebula

She (I'll call her "she") rears up
from the black cloud of gas and dust
that slides in and hides her back and flanks
but sketches the great profile in charcoal.

She's magnificent, her unseen hind
legs and hoofs lifting her
in space, dusky eye a-glint,
her unseen mane on the other side.

She carries the universe on her back.
Her unseen rider grips her chest
between his legs. Their journey's protracted
and shared. She calms under his caress.

Bipolar Nebulae

One wonders if they stay awake all night
composing poems. And are their down days dark
as Hadean shades? So that they swallow pills
to sleep by day? And do they run up bills
they cannot pay and recklessly have sex
with strangers, thinking they have found true love?

But no. I've let myself be carried away.
Bipolar nebulae result from a type
of topography: a bulge beneath spreading
the nebulae wide, like two breathing lungs.
Or wings: because a ghostly butterfly
overlays the image of nebulae.

Andromeda

Sometimes a child outwits her crummy parents.
Andromeda, for instance. Born to a vain,
narcissistic mother who declared
herself (not her daughter!) "the fairest of all,
prettier than the Nereids," which slur
upon his own daughters seriously miffed
Poseidon, the Nereids' dad, who quickly dispatched
a monster to ravage coast and city. Now
Andromeda's father, the king, was frantic. What
to do? The oracle advised the king
to sacrifice a virgin, who happened to be—
Andromeda. O those tragic Greeks!
The king ordered his daughter chained unclothed
to a rock in the treacherous sea. But bold Perseus,
returning from battle with the Gorgon Medusa,
saw the naked princess struggling against her chains,
grew hot and rescued her and then, Dear Reader,
married her. After a long, fulfilling life
Andromeda died. Athena set her in the heavens,
a jewel among jewels, a diadem of diamonds,
next to the constellations of her much-loved husband
and stupidly superficial but, yes, dear mother,
Cassiopeia, who'd none of her daughter's virtuous,
uncomplaining courage. Pitied her mother, did
Andromeda, for wanting compliments to bolster
her against the awful onslaught of increasing age,
that ogre who bullies women into self-shame
and fear of divorce and acrid loneliness,
that ogre who snorts like a pig, blames women
for being—what? Why, who they are. Themselves.
Andromeda is a blueshifted galaxy,

destined (we think) to collide with the Milky Way
in roughly 4.5 billion years.
Meanwhile beautiful Andromeda
sleeps beside her husband in a bed of stars.

A Dialogue between Mars and Venus

FIRST SPEAKER

The two attendant moons, Fear and Dread,
float face up in your "canals" like bloated fish, reflected.
I dredge them up like old boots,
wave arms and bluster as you will.
I catch; *I* don't kill.
Now why are you turning red?
See here, General, that high color is a warning signal,
to watch your heart.

SECOND SPEAKER

I would watch yours.
You hide your heart
beneath thick clouds—
your rock heart.
Oh yes, the astronomer loves the hours
he lives in Palomar's dome.
You are his one home,
and mine.

The World as Hologram

A new hypothesis suggests
that we are holograms, vessels
of light projected from a plane
at the edge of a black hole.

In short, we're software, down to our toes,
our tics and quirks programmed. God knows
what this might mean. If anything.
If meaning still has meaning.

Is the world no more than *maya*, then,
its appearance not to be trusted?
But isn't that what some of us,
leery as hell, had thought before

this new hypothesis appeared?
Well, then, no need for anger or
despair: nothing has changed.
Nothing is weirder than it was.

Blowback

Rich and strange as a sea-change is outer space,
where energetic electrons blown back to earth
pitch streams of ionized gas toward the poles.
If such a stream breaks off, electrons surge
into the poles' magnetic fields and light
up: aurora borealis and
aurora australis, the northern and the southern.

I saw the aurora borealis as
a child in Ithaca, the vast night sky
on fire with greens and pinks and blue-based maroons.
My father had buttoned tight my winter coat.
In pockets, my hands were warm. The burning sky
behind the tenement in which we lived
swallowed stars like popcorn at the movies.

And what a movie it was.

Occam's Razor

Imagine a point of unimaginable density.
This is where we begin, without dimension,
timeless and solitary. What causes the point
to break into countless pieces? We might as well
ask what breaks the human heart: every
thing and no one thing.
                          The pieces coalesce
or sail through space, perhaps creating it
in their wake. Gases mutate into stars
and rocks crash headlong into one another,
becoming planets gravitationally mustered
into orbits around the boiling suns, solar
systems eloping with galaxies, perhaps
honeymooning along event horizons,
those seductive portals to black holes, points
of unimaginable density.
                          You've heard
of Occam's Razor. Well, one thinks it may
be smarter to believe the Christian myth
than tales of gravity so great that light
cannot escape and strings that twist and loop
into other universes, and time itself
an old-timey flipbook of static scenes.

Astronomer and Telescope

He talks to it. It speaks to him
of distance and embargoed freight,
the beltway asteroids, the kami-
kaze comets and all the other
furnishings afloat in outer space
and as he listens, he is lulled
to sleep by the oldest tale of all,
the one about the stillness of
eternity and how it brought
into being time, and all
the creatures of time, unfolding life,
the sky spreading light lavishly
everywhere.
                Eternity
was bored. Grew restless in its chains,
desired to shake them off and see
the world. An urge natural
enough, considering electrons.
Considering particle physics.
Which required considering time,
according to Albert Einstein.
Now there was a *now*, and then
a *then*, *before*, and *after*, and
a *during*. Babies grew into
adolescents and then adults.
And then—and then!—began to die.
An insignificant fall, a slip
off the curb, the lingering cough, the sense
of a bumptious lump in a breast once pert,
the ache in the bone, the stiffness in
the joint. We die in increments.

(Maybe not all of us, but most
of us anyway, parts breaking
down like outdated machinery.)

But look—the scientist's awake,
his nap completed. What a dream
he had, high up on his telescope.
There was—there was—but what was it
he dreamed? Electrons, ticking clocks—
and now he's angry with himself
for wasting observational time,
expensive as it is and hard
to get. The lines! The lists of scientists!
And yet the dream . . . the dream moving
farther away with each minute
that passes. . . . Oh, why can he not call
the dream to mind? Perhaps it made
no sense. Few dreams do, he thinks,
unless we piece the wisps of them
together like a Freudian
and he is not a Freudian;
rather, an astronomer
who seized forty winks while the heavens and earth
accepted their places in the scheme of things.

Everything Lifted Off from the Earth

Everything lifted off from the earth.
Trees rose into the clouds, their roots trailing like bridal trains.
Buildings drifted starward.
A stampede of palominos flashed across the sky.

Then the people let go of whatever had held them back
and rose up, some slowly, some faster,
so that it was not unusual to pass or be passed by a friend or enemy,
but conversation confined itself to pleasantries.

The planet itself moved off its orbit, and many were afraid
that it might roll after them and knock them down like
bowling pins,
but it dropped away in the opposite direction, becoming ever smaller,
a tumbleweed, a softball,

and the people kept leapfrogging into space
as if they were headed for heaven.

II

Cogitation

To think is to be, said Descartes,
but maybe not, maybe to be
is to think, or so it seems to me,
though Blaise Pascal's intentional heart
adds yet another dimension to
what was two-dimensional:
We live our lives in 3-D, all
we think and are, blind and askew.

Memories

They come, they go,
leaving behind a trail
of blue smoke, blue
because they are often sad,
smoke, because that's what
they do, lounging against store fronts,
waiting for you to remember
to pick them up.
And when you do
they hop into the back seat,
saying *Drive faster,* or
Let's stop by Miranda's house,
do you remember her?

Riga 1975

I knew you then. You were a man jealous
of freedom, firmly believing in everyone's right
to it: freedom to say what needed saying,
to do what needed doing— to make music, love.
Hemlock and toothpick pine punctured the sky
as we drove north toward the blue Baltic, which cools
and pales as autumn begins, and autumn always
begins soon, oak leaves riding stiff currents
like seagulls or ospreys, swooping, circling, diving
to the muddy bottom of the endless sky.
When I remember you, the earth turns over.
Time becomes vertiginous, the past
present, the future foretold so long ago
that by now we have forgotten our common fate.

Remember those trees, how sunlight burst from their branches
like cherry blossoms in spring, though fall was on its way,
the Baltic blue but fading to gray.

Reverie

When one is on the verge of sleep but not
sleeping and not exactly daydreaming either
and diverse images enter the mind without
invitation but also without presumption,
we call that reverie, though Buddhist monks
might call it meditation, Zen awareness.
The images are comforting or not,
terrifying perhaps, but stream across
one's mind like light across the universe,
screening what is there though it is so
far away it cannot be pertinent—
it's in the past even while it's present.
Ease into it. Discover how the flow
carries you away. Merrily you go.

Imagination

Imagination is the wildest wind,
blows us where we never guessed we'd go.
The Thessaly of long ago, perhaps,
its incense overpowering, so that we reel
as if drunk on wine or ouzo. As if sirens
sang us into a spell of longing so
intense it yanked us off a well-trod path.

Or Roman Britain, with its chunk-stone fences
and military outposts guarded by
guys who thought their country ruled the world
and always would. In this and many other
ways, America emulates the Rome
of former times but now think yourself there,
inhaling cooking smells pervading streets

and alleys. Or imagine China, the future
awaiting all of us, economists say,
though I imagine a future farther away—
another planet or galaxy, where
the water's clean, the atmosphere pure,
and all the forms of life live peaceably
and not one has to eat any other one.

Imagination is imagination,
alas, and not reality and yet
its force outstrips the force of a tornado.
That which we imagine may lead us to
improve our world or country or city
or maybe only the room we occupy,
but that, as people say, is a beginning.

In an Alternate World

(If Wittgenstein, Popper, and Freud Had Met in Vienna in 1932)

The disputatious regulars who met
each night in echoey Viennese cafes
pronounced upon philosophy and art,
on economics and the efficacy
of modern science. Smoke clouded the ceiling,
the clattering of coffee cups another
less argumentative conversation.

Was language a reflection of the world
asked one. Another said that language makes
the world, or fixes it in time. A third
insisted instability's the essence
of language. Ludwig Wittgenstein likened language
to games. But Popper wouldn't play, and Freud
spun mythy stories from meaningless slips of tongue.

They nodded, quarreled, huffed and puffed until
the owner of the place had swept them out
onto the cold, dark streets. The stars were crisp,
defined, as clear as thought itself might be,
if only thought were clear. Young Wittgenstein
saw the problem clearly. He blew his nose
into the large white lily of his handkerchief.

And all this thought, this clever argument,
where did it lead? Perhaps, as Thomas Mann
would have it in *The Magic Mountain*, to
the individual, distinctive yet
blurred and disappearing into the future,
becoming lost among the very many,
becoming, at the last, nothing but language.

Seemingly Enigmatic

Beneath the propositions and assertions
we make each day lie not just rules of grammar
but hidden logic, the gangly hanging skeleton
a breath-filled life embraces. Thus logicians
are orthopedists of the thinking mind.
They sometimes break a patient's leg to heal it.
A metaphorical leg, of course, as "patient"
refers to paradox, and paradox
is a paralysis of cogitation.
But what of metaphor and simile,
the ways in which a poem or story speaks?
Do not they have their own hidden logic?
In them, paradox perambulates
then makes an end run around the law of non-contradiction.

On the Perception of Time

According to the latest thinking, time
perceived may hang on well-nigh imperceptible
neurotransmitters tucked away in differing
cranial regions. Thus time does not so much
flow like a river as signal like the signal
man of an earlier day: start, stop, slow, fast,
wait. Switch tracks. You cannot step into
the same river twice, said Heraclitus,
but now you cannot step into it once
as the river no longer flows. We might decide
to think of time as the signalman, waltzing
with his flags, the locomotive adding on
luxury cars or leaving others behind,
warning whistle haunting a night-hid landscape.

Patterning

In constellations and the butterfly's wings
we locate patterns, for we are locators
of pattern in everything: the mind revealed
in action or a lack of action, legal
history, physics and poetry, whatever
we can think of, as patterning is how we think.

Or might it be the way that Nature thinks?

I think of Esther Conwell, physicist,
who fathoms "transport charges in DNA,"
and tracks the effect of "strong fluctuations"
on "the motion of the polarons," and though
I do not understand a word of what
she does, I know that writers, also, track

fluctuations and those fluctuations
will map a metaphor or inscribe images
as vivid and vibrant with movement as Matisse
or Klee or a musical phrase by Wolfgang Mozart.
Her husband, Abraham Rothberg, as a boy
a cantor, tenor, wrote a choir of books

in which he traced the fluctuations of
the heart and mind and soul and society,
the manic history of the twentieth century,
its wars and lies and convulsive politics,
but also praised the values of freedom and choice
for all. And what a pattern freedom makes,

the sky a canvas on which cumulus clouds
stacked like ziggurats collide with a blue
as high and wide as Shamayim might be, if
there were a heaven, a beachhead heaven in which
wisps of cirrus curl and float and fade
as the Righteous Dead seek a cooling shade.

The Nature of Hypothesis

Experiment and draft are much alike,
trying out this idea and that.
Scientists proceed by hypothesis—
asserting that a statement is the case,
testing the truth of it afterward.
And just so proceeds the artful poet
or should we say the heartful poet, given
that the poet says what he knows and loves.

But as we have to wait to know the truth,
we have to wait as long to know a poem
or song is worthy. Thus Shakespeare and Bach,
their sonnets and sonatas, waited in
the wings, lost from history for a time,
a painful thought but one that's true. And yet
our hypothesis— *their art was true*
and beautiful—is seen at last to have
been valid all along, the words of Shakespeare
as measured as *armonia,* his casts
of characters contrapuntal, Bach's sonatas
a series of poetic interpretations
of sound and of the astounding world of the mind.
Or rather, Shakespeare's words are music sublime
and Bach's sonatas monologues of light.

Metaphor as Method

I value logic and empiricism
and cherish scientific method for
the knowledge it uncovers but I love
the leap across a chasm that is metaphor.

To find a similarity between
two disparate things reveals that all
is one, and one reflects the all there is.
A metaphor unites the world, whereas
government does not, and metaphor
expands the mind, as deduction doesn't.

In adolescence I drew a downward line
on a ruled page, one side headed Logic,
the other Analogic. It seemed to me
both were ways of thinking and if I was
wrong, one must admit a metaphor
is by far the shortest distance between two points.

On Intuition

Not thought of as a rational resource,
our intuition warrants real respect
for saving us from countless calamities.
And then there are uncanny moments when
an unarticulated feeling nudges
the mind toward what it does not know it knows.
Perhaps it guides your hand toward Bonhoeffer;
you pull it from your shelves of books, a book
you have not read, and as you draw it down
you feel the goodness of the man as if
he shares this room, this small room lighted by
a study lamp and three small, screened windows
and the bright, unburning blaze that flares up from
pages in which the pastor, stripped naked,
condemned to die by hanging, kneels and prays.

Invention

Necessity is not its only mother.
Sheer boredom also has a role to play.
Idle hands working insensible clay—
not always wasted effort. And another
thing: curiosity will motivate
the idlest of us to intensest study.
The doctor cannot resist the human body.
The publicist must publicize the private.

The novelist surmises what comes next.
The scientist cannot resist testing
her theory. Curious, they push on, through
obstacles, past wrong turns, wanting answers
to their endless questions. Such passion is arresting,
and transforms daily stasis to connection.

On Mathematical Logic

Mathematical logic is beautiful.
Maybe you don't agree?
But logic cuts out all the folderol,
allowing us to see

clearly the terms of argument, with no
extraneous considerations.
A proposition states the status quo,
unaffected by sensation

or emotion or even appetite
and, we hope, desire,
though what logician does not invite
a clarifying fire

to burn the dross, to blaze a signal path
through synapse and syntax
and embrace the classic loveliness of math,
so elegant, and immodestly bared of facts.

Consilience

It means to bring together two conclusions
reached by different systems of thought.
                                          Ergo,
a line of poetry, when set to music,
combusts as lieder, perhaps by Franz Schubert.
To those who use the word, this example
may seem a mere frivolity—but only
if they've not heard Fischer-Dieskau singing
Die schöne Müllerin or *Winterreise,*
nor known the comfort and companionship
a song can lend a soul. Consilience
will find a way when other ways cannot.

Contemplation as Complication

To question is the basic mode of thought.
Those bright lights in the night sky—what are they?
And who are we? And where are we? And why
are living creatures made to die?

Questions lead to questions; it's guaranteed.
And some of them get answered lickety-split,
but others we have to ask again and again.
This, too, is part of the plan.

What plan? The plan to make us think.
The plan to make us smarter than we are.
To question is to complicate the case
like adding ferns to flowers in a vase.

Fog at Emerald Isle, North Carolina

Fog slips in from the south, takes out the horizon.
The white horses of the sea shake their manes.
Out of darkness, nothing. Out of light, nothing.
Silenced with great age. A view of America before it was America.
Time so slow its heart beats once in a century.
The tide an uneven hem dragging in the back.
Sea oats in lieu of a fence.
Cloud butterflies surveilling the area.
Yucca plants like sentries.
Shells scattered on the shore like spent bullets.
Feel the salted air, taste it, smell.
Can you find the seagull?
The footsteps?
Signs of a struggle?

We Pray for These and All

worms that plow the earth
minerals buried dark-deep in time
reclusive fossils and those
that never formed—life
that left no mark, none
not even a signature X

we pray for these and all
other vanished unknown things

the twisted roots of elderly trees
water sliding underground
aurochs; early humans who traced
their open hands on cave walls cool
as moss and dank with moist air
urns embracing handfuls of dust

we pray for these and all
vanished, vanishing, and to vanish

and what of words,
those fair-weather friends,
those light-as-nothing syllables
lifted on a wave
across the expanding universe
and gone?

We pray for the unseen, the unfound, the disappeared.
Not to retrieve but to acknowledge.

Absence

Of existential terrors, I think the most
terrifying has to be the absence
of oneself from almost every moment in
the infinite series of moments that is time.
You were not there for Plato's lectures nor
in Mexico with Trotsky, and the poems
of Li Po were written without your help.
Nor did the world await the advent of you.

How long before the boiling oceans cooled,
before the funky trilobite could crawl
and bright skies darkened, the atmosphere roiled
by pterodactyls' proto-wings? Time is
a form of vertigo, as if we looked
downward from an insensible height into
a well without a bottom. Then our own
wee bit, or brief newsbite, of time arrives
and in less of it than an eye-blink takes
leave, and with it, our generation departs
(already some have left) and we shall be
a long time gone, a long time without time.

To face infinity is to stand in a strong wind
that cannot distinguish between you and a tree
or rock or blade of grass or roof or brick
or fence or phone pole or snapped branch or stick.

To face infinity is to be cut down
to size, the infinitesimal speck of dust
that is yourself, indistinguishable
from any other speck of musty dust.

Small Errors with Gigantic Consequences

I speak of the smallest errors,
the ones that, lined up, spell catastrophe:
A minute error in measurement, meteor
that was supposed to miss but scalded Siberia.
A planned bomb-radius that failed to stick
to the plan. An unnoticed miscalculation
in bridge construction that resulted in
the deaths of a dozen unsuspecting people.

A teller makes a small mistake that leads
to another and that leads to another and next
you know, the bank is plumb out of money.
Or should we blame the lenient loan officer?
Both routes come to the same—disaster, like a clot
in the brain, abrupt and lethal, or the butterfly
whose tremulous wings unhinge the seven seas
from continents, blue drowning its sister, green.

To please a special friend, you made a necklace
out of string and sea glass. You wrapped your gift
in wrapping paper with hand-painted butterflies.
The string broke, the sea glass shattered, and
there was nothing you could say but "I'm sorry."

The Dog of Brownian Motion

It happens everywhere, on every scale
from microscopic to the universal:
things fluctuate. The very air that seems
as still as the inside of an empty jar
is massively excited by batallions
of particles. Or think of matter as
an aerobics class, a gym where molecules
work out. Or think of Sufis dancing or
anyone dancing. Think of molecules bandied
about like shuttlecocks. By now you have
the picture, a universal trembling that
elicits sympathy and a desire
to hold the whole damn thing as close to us
as possible, to give it food and water
and a warm, comfortable place to sleep at night.

Quanta

Things quanta are too small to see
and pop up everywhere,
including here, including there,
including here-and-there.

Shrödinger's cat's alive or dead
or both, and we won't know
which until we open the box
whereupon she will be dead

or alive. Things get so entangled
when they are quanta and so
decoherent when they are not.
I like to think of Shrödinger's cat

licking her paws, her small pink tongue
busy and fussy, her tail
coiled self-protectively: a cat
ready for what comes.

Atomism

Democritus hypothesized a world
composed of atoms, invisible particles
that he imagined as miniscule building blocks,
rather like Legos, perhaps, or Tinker Toys.
An interesting theory, not right, but
not altogether wrong.
                        What interests *me:*
the underlying, unstated assumption that
large gestures need to be supported by
more modest ones. Is this a principle
of engineering? No one wants the bridge
to buckle, collapsing beneath the weight of wartime
refugees in flight.
                 Or consider the symphonies
of Gustave Mahler, the sweeping themes to inter-
stellar space stretched.
                       To build a world or bridge
or major symphonic masterwork requires
acquaintance with the load-bearing wall,
abundance of musical ideas, and
a grasp of the moments that construct the hour,
the day, the scores on scores on scores of years.

The God Particle

I
The scientists who work with quantum mechanics
despise the term "god particle," assigned
by overdramatic media to the as-yet
hypothetical Higgs boson, the which,
if it exists, lends mass to every scrap
of matter in the universe. Without
mass, there would be no universe.
Hence, the importance of the Higgs boson
and the reason for its promotion to "God particle,"
but one is well behooved to remember that
the Higgs boson is not omnipotent
or omniscient or omnipresent and
has yet to make any appearance at all
and if it does,
                will be vanishingly small.

II
And now they think they've found it, the which without,
no thing is more than nothing. Consequently
(for there are always consequences), our cosmos
teeters on the edge of dissolution, leans
more toward this than that, partial to
a certain part of the whole.
                        Whole what?
                                Shebang.
A radical instability, manifest
in the Higgs, suggests the universe may end
at any moment. An antimatter bubble

could tunnel through the universe, disrupting
time and space. It could be happening now
and we are in the dark about it, because
time can't go faster than the speed of light,
and if it does get here, it will arrive
at the speed of light—too fast for us to see it.
All gone, then, the lot of us. All gone the stars,
the countless worlds. The laws of physics? Maybe.
All gone the which without which nothing is.

Heaven on Earth

Integument and sheath, a human being
provides a perfect home for microscopic
parasites who've found their paradise.
They feed on us with avidity
and maybe with a sense of gratitude,
the germ in the gut growing as fat as fat,
glistening in bile or blood like a recovered fortune,
a mite in eye or ear like a displaced small child
seeking refuge from the rabid wildlife
rampant upon even the mildest body.
We think ourselves, ourselves, but we are many
and do not know all who inhabit the heaven—
haven—that flourishes between our toes
or nest in the hairs of our fine Roman nose.

Demodex Folliculorum

A kind of mite comes out at night to skate
our eyeballs. Eyelids shuttered, we're oblivious.
The monster-mites do triple Lutzes, spin in place
on one skate or two or eight and still they fail
to win awards for an Olympiad
without judges. Yet win they should, because
their sowchows, flips, and loops, jumps, and axels
revitalize our eyes, scour the rink
(no roses left on artificial ice),
Hoover up anything irrelevant
or in the way. Every day we wake
to a world as newly bright as a starry night
illumined by candles stuck in van Gogh's hat.

Regarding Clouds

Bacteria and fungi fly
upward, seeding clouds.
Not all clouds, but some.
And then the clouds precipitate,

bacteria and fungi falling
down to earth.
A simple explanation for
the birth and death of clouds,
the rise and fall of clouds,
the being and nonbeing of clouds,

those irrepressible bacteria,
those wily fungi.

In the Desert

In the desert, shadow is a function of wind.
The wind blows, and dust devils cleanse
light-colored surface particles such as silt,
dust and clay from what becomes—seen
distantly—dark ephemeral trails across sand.
This map leads nowhere—to an oasis perhaps
or the mirage of an oasis, water
blue as a Broadway musical,
palms ripe with dates, a modest breeze
to cool your sweat-beaded brow.
But mirages are for suckers, you know that.
You turn your back upon illusion and
the shifting sands, the shadows that come and go,
shield your eyes, and go slow, slow.

The Wind

We read it in the trees, the clouds,
the curtains: a nearly sentient breeze

ambitious to seize the world
and shake it by the shoulders.

We read it in the clouds
that shoulder through the sky

as if the world's a way
station to pass by.

We read it in the leaves
outflanked and fallen, bodies

on a battlefield after the fact,
the land a wasted tract.

We read it in our clothes:
the willful skirt, the woman's

long hair whipping around her face
on a windy day in any place.

And think, too, of solar
wind in outer space.

DNA

We scale a winding staircase
or swinging ladder like Jacob's
in the Bible as if we might
ascend to eternity,

a state in which we'll be
bionic and brainier,
with silicon chips. We'll be
a new species: *Homo*

Wikipediens,
our minds digitalized,
able to access all
information and

we'll persist forever,
or anyhow, not be dead,
not quite, though without
time, it must be said,

we also won't be alive.
Yes, if you're nostalgic
you may seek to disembark
from evolution, but

first, ask yourself whether
your child and spouse deserve
protection from disease,
death, and accident,

or can you let them go,
unique as they are,
irreplaceable,
into a place darker

than shadow?

Negative Numbers

If we assign to all the dead
one negative integer each,
the sum would be so far below
the number one, I would not dare
to eat a peach, or subtract.
And what about infinite sets
that are greater or smaller
but equally infinite?
Or are they merely approximate?
I read Russell and Whitehead
so long ago they seem to me
as imaginary as imaginary
integers and yet they opened
a highway in the mind that led
to infinity.

Radiation

"Zone of alienation," they designate
the area around Chernobyl, where
after thirty years, some life's come back
to life: a kind of tree, a kind of bird,
but resurrection is contingent and
tentative here, where radiation seeps
into marsh and air and wood, where radiation
burns silently and with great secretiveness
in humans, trees, and animals and plants,
mutation in the blood, in DNA,
familiar, friendly cells combusting jar-
ringly like bombs concealed in low-profile
packages.
          The packages are people, of course,
people contained in their protective but porous
skin, that sweet and salty, sometimes bruised
casing that tells us where we start and stop
in space. Without that basic information
we might lose our places and, confused, occupy
already occupied spaces, causing
much merriment and no little dismay,
depending on how you interpret the situation.

But no—the situation is too sad,
too final, to recast as farce or romance.
Albino swallows dip and soar above
nuclear waste facilities, and lynx
and boar roam the radioactive wilds.
Nuclear reactor number 4 is interred
within a cracked concrete sarcophagus.

So will the name "Alienation Zone"
be latterly attached to Fukushima,
that prefecture in northern Japan where earth-
quake and tsunami ravaged a power plant?
Biocontamination is the word
we use when milk or vegetables or anything
living absorbs radioactive fallout.

Marie Skłodowska Curie, as passionate
about her work as about the men she loved
(and there were several, smart and handsome),
tucked test tubes of radioactive isotopes
in her skirt pocket and in her desk drawer,
delighting in the glow they emitted
in the dark. Over time—what little was left—
her body became a zone of alienation.

Light

Inside the sea are shifting shallows of light,
the darkling undertow, by contrast, light
as anything that's not nailed down. The light—
photons—is less than lightweight, hence, light.

The surface of the sea: scintillas of light
like a corps de ballet, en pointe dancers as light
on their feet in their Moira Shearer shoes as light
on air. A question neither idle nor light:

Are ballerinas weightless, quite like light?
Is light what we see or what allows us to see? Is light
the opposite or absence of dark? Is light
a function of motion? What, then, is light?

Dark Energy

The process whereby cosmic materiél
collects could be, perhaps, called *cosmosis*,
stuff swallowing stuff, and in a way, that's true
though it's more accurate to say that some
thing unseen is pushing everything
apart, which leaves each cut cross-section of
the universe with only a little bit
of matter and a huge amount of space,
the sky dead black excepting a few faint flourishes
of starlight from so long ago we'd need
a lifetime simply to count the years it took
to reach us on our aging earth, by now
hotter than Hades as our giant red sun
swallows the tasty amuse-bouche of us.

IV

Childhood and God

Each night at dusk the deer return, noiseless,
to eat the juicy apples in the orchard:
a buck, a doe or two, and slender fawns.
We've given up trying to keep them out.
They merge into the branches, fading light,
dying summer grass, the gravel drive.
We know them only by their absence, which
is also how we know childhood and God.

Childhood and God: Vacation Bible School
in summer, where each day each student recited
a Bible verse. *Jesus saves* was popular.
On our heads, Christian beanies, even though
our parents were skeptical. A teacher taught
us how to make a handbag from white cloth
and string, and you could loop the string around
your small wrist to let the handbag dangle.

I loved to let the drawstring handbag dangle.
I loved to say the Bible verses daily.
I thought I loved God, but I was skeptical.
Perhaps I knew him by his gaping absence.
Perhaps by summer's end he had noiselessly merged
into the branches, fading light, dying.
I kept the handbag in my dresser drawer
for years before I finally threw it away.

Conscience

Not everybody has one, but most do,
and those who have one have to live with it,
this constant partner who can be glum or resentful
or covered in shame and difficult to console.

Reconciliation with one's conscience
requires apology and amendment.
It is the duty of one beset by bad
conscience to repair the damage, rotten cad

that he is. And knows he is, because conscience
tells him so. If we could temper our dismay,
would conscience release us from its too-tight grasp?
Would conscience lose its frown? See the light of day?

Complicity

Days implicate us in their myriad doings.
The crime is ours and time's. The punishment?
Death by foul or any means. We meant,

no doubt, to do our best, be true to life
and art, to celebrate the mind and heart.
Time interferes, takes intention apart,

a crucial bolt or nut left lying on
the floor beneath a covered couch or chair.
We never fail to fail. It's never there,

that bolt or nut, that Phillips screw or socket.
The passing days will close the door and lock it
before we reinvent ourselves. People

inclined to religion might say our complicity
with time is the original "original sin."
Corruption happens everywhere and when.

Snow in Southwest Minnesota

In southwest Minnesota snow's the crop
of every field, every bush, every
dirt road and tree. Fences lie buried beneath
it. Students maze their way through underground
tunnels to math classes and dormitories.
The sun, a broken, burnt-out bulb, cannot
defrost the sky or thaw ten thousand lakes
and there's no horizon: the horizon's blotted
out. I taught there though I also was a
student (the only way I could get housing
on campus, which I had to have because
I didn't drive). And if I'd had a car
wouldn't I have driven into a snowbank,
given white-out conditions, which we were?
I took a class in relativity
and learned that tachyons are hypothetical
particles moving faster than light. If such
phenomena existed they would have
imaginary mass but since they don't
exist they must have . . . imaginary mass?

The Visitors

The light was off, the room black-dark.
In black-dark, the bedroom filled
with the shapes and selves of those I'd known
when they were living. Slowly they filed

past me—mother, father, brother
and friends, the friends of a lifetime
and others I'd known for the length of a reading
or conference or academic term.

So many gone. They pressed so close
to the bed I thought I might be crushed.
I switched the night lamp on: the room,
as empty as air, was bright and hushed.

Their Pleas

They pluck my sleeve, tug my hand, pull
my hair. They do not kneel to kiss my hem.
No, it's not like that but they want tokens.
Again, not souvenirs but something small
and useful, something that will help them out
after life, maybe in an underworld.
They need a sighted guide to lead them to
the river, and they need a remnant of
the old world as they embark for the older world,
the one that has existed since the first
grievous death. They need to feel they still
can touch and still be touched, as once they did
and were, and one would have to be a cold,
uncaring woman to deny their pleas:
a woman with a bullet-proof heart,
without a memory of life on earth.

They Are More Present

They are more present to me now, perhaps,
than when they were alive, my family
of father, mother, brother. In my dreams
they visit me, distressed and wanting help,
lonely and wanting a little company.
My mother has financial problems, is
running out of the money she had saved.
Father has forgotten how to play
the Bach Chaconne and tears his hair out
as if beneath it he will find the mind
he's lost. My brother wants to marry me,
but dead he cannot do this and he weeps
and drinks, forgetting that he's wanted to wed
every woman he ever met. I hear
their importunings, their wails and lamentations.
O friend, please put your hands over my ears.
I hear. I hear my dear ones' piteous cries.

Looking for My Dead Mother's Phone Number

I was looking for my dead mother's phone number.
If I couldn't call her, I'd have no address to give
the taxi driver. I had no money for a plane
ticket. I had no correct change for the bus
that would have taken me to the airport if
it hadn't gone the long way around, which meant
I wound up missing everything. Besides,
there was too much baggage to handle by myself.
Someone said, "You can't take it with you," but
I needed my books, my frocks, my curve-hugging,
floor-length evening gown, my financial records,
and my black Reeboks. I'd stuffed my stuff into boxes
that kept coming open, the contents kept spilling out.
I grabbed my savings passbook and raced panting
for the plane. First, there was the house to go
through (not ours) with dark, narrow staircases that led
to the basement, except there were no stairs. One had
to slide down. It was very tricky. My little
sister was with me. I was holding her hand
until I realized I wasn't and ran back
and found her in the soda shop. She had
almost disappeared, like the rest of our family.
We crouched in the hallway and I held her in
my arms. My sister was six years old with
golden cornsilk hair and a missing front tooth
for which the tooth fairy had left her a nickel.
She was scared but she trusted me. Why?
Why did my sister trust me? When I knew nothing?
Nothing, nothing, nothing. Nothing. Nothing.

An Apology

How late I was to learn I loved my sister.
How inexcusable, my stupid mistake.
And how does a person make such a stupid mistake?
The members of a family will form
alliances to strengthen their positions
even though position will shift and shift
and shift again, the starry constellations
changing with the seasons of the earth.
Thus, time passes and an old woman knows
the younger sister who tagged after her,
so gratified simply to stand in her shadow,
was sweet as all get-out and smarter than
the sister who too seldom held her hand.

The Cliffs of Nothingness

We hiked out to find them.
It took, you understand, a long time.
Long enough to whittle my husband lean.
But his legs ached and his hip hurt.
For me, it was my knees.
My knees were about as functional as two doughnuts with sprinkles!

We lost count of the stars and galaxies we passed,
the worlds, the *devastating infinities*,
to repurpose a phrase. Unwillingly, we acquired
canes and glasses but we were determined,
and we prevailed, although by the end
we were nearly dead with exhaustion.

A wind from nowhere forced us back from the edge;
it chiseled our faces featureless
and still we persisted. How could we not?
We always wanted to know what could be known
and besides, what choice did we have?
There was nowhere to turn back to.

Thus we withstood the wind and looked over
the edge. Indeed, *there* was nothing.
The sight of it shocked us into silence.
Had we become so much smaller,
or was nothingness the whole of everything?
Well. It defeated us—that much nothingness.

Even if we could have returned, we were too tired.
We spread out our sleeping bag
designed for two. Shielded from the wind,
cozied in goosedown and shared body heat,
we held hands. Now the wind passed over us
as if it had a more important objective,

some deadline to meet.
My husband began to laugh,
not loudly. By now I was rather deaf
but he shouted in my ear: "It was
a fine walk! A fine long walk!"
I squeezed his skeleton hand.

Of Love and Time

Time felt expands and shrinks according to
the number of details that we observe.
The less familiar an experience,
the more details we notice, lengthening
the time it takes; and the more ordinary,
the fewer details adhere. And yet your face,
better known to me than is my name,
and creased and folded like a well-used map,
is a place in which I'd live a million years
if I could, every year a century,

every century a millennium

and all that lengthy while I'll register
the play of light upon your light green eyes,
silver stubble and mobile mouth, the way
you clear your throat to say a thing clever
or punning. Such minute observations
to me are Shakespearian dramaturgy
and bespeak a narrative of close detail
that makes each single moment as riveting
as insight and as lingering as a poem
about the inexhaustible theme of love.

The Loneliness of the Human Being

I see by your face
that you are sad
or happy or troubled
or psychotically mad,

or do I misjudge?
Perhaps you've adopted
a face to meet mine,
as Eliot said?

I can only guess
and must guess wrong
at least some of the time.
There's surely a song

about the distance
between us two
even when I'm
in your purview

and you in mine.

Dear, even when
you hold me tight
I can't be sure
I read you right.

Geophysics

Geophysics maps our singular globe—
molten lava here, falling water there,
rocks, moraines, and minerals everywhere.

I thought I'd be a lunarologist—
a word I'd coined myself—transporting my "skills"
to the bleakly bland surface of the moon.

Without an atmosphere to block my view
I'd see stars so alarmingly bright they startled me,
but would their constellations be the same

as on earth. Would manly Orion snatch a nap
in Cassiopeia's chair? The North Star drift
southward to the Antilles? Would the bearer

of water flood not the Nile but the Potomac?
In the meantime, at New Mexico Tech scads
and scads of scientists studied thunderstorms,

with a heavy emphasis on lightning strikes
and supercells. But who would ask to be
electrocuted, even in the name of Nature?

Not I, I must admit. And so I quit
trying to become a lunarologist,
which, after all, didn't even exist,

and moved on to philosophy, my first and deepest
love except of course for writing, which
I loved even before I figured out

that one could make up stuff. The Palmer Method
was purely satisfying from the letter A.
So let the geophysicists do what

they do: geophysics. I am glad
they tell us stories about our whirling earth.
They read its past, decipher its likely future

should we have a future, and help us understand
phenomena that spooked our ancestors.
And I am also glad not to be

a member of the tribe, for I belong
indoors, writing the letter A and scores
more?

The Studio

Light fell in by way of two windows
tall enough to stand in.
The green hills of Auvillar
slanted back from the restraining wall.
Magpies and butterflies:
artwork on the wing.
A dog barked, a rooster crowed.

By evening,
she had got from her brain
what it had to give.
Each morning she began again.

We live a mysterious life
in a mysterious setting
on the outskirts of the Milky Way,
and the light from two windows
is enough to clarify
the limits of clarity.

The Right Words

An oblong of white light
on the studio wall,
green and yellow leaves
seen through glass panes
of the studio door.

Skylight. Chairs. Lamps.

The words are here, too,
but less apparent.
I must look for them
by daylight or lamplight,
stay put, observe.

Acknowledgments

Aethlon: "Demodex Folliculorum"; *Alhambra Poetry Calendar* (Belgium): "Invention"; *Arts and Letters:* "The Cliffs of Nothingness" and "They Are More Present"; *Asheville Poetry Review:* "Fog at Emerald Island, North Carolina"; *The Broadkill Review:* "Astronomer and Telescope" and "In an Alternate World"; *Cave Wall:* "Of Stars" (first published as "Stars"); *Connotations:* "Paradox"; *Cutthroat:* "The Dog of Brownian Motion"; *Hartskill Review:* "Reverie" and "On Mathematical Logic"; "Consilience" and "Negative Numbers"; "Snow in Southwest Minnesota"; *In Other Words, Meridá* (now *The Merida Review*): "Alice These Days," "Andromeda," "On the Perception of Time," and "Regarding Clouds," http://www.inotherwordsmerida.com; *International Poetry Review:* "Riga, 1975"; *Kenyon Review:* "Radiation" and "Geophysics"; *Lake City Lights:* "Bipolar Nebulae" and "Contemplation as Complication"; *Literature and Belief:* "The Studio"; *Literary Imagination:* "Childhood and God"; *Literary Matters:* "Occam's Razor," "Imagination," and "The Nature of Hypothesis"; *Measure:* "Musica Universalis"; also, "Music and Mathematics" and "The Loneliness of the Human Being"; also, "Quanta"; *Per Contra:* "Memories"; "Cogitation," "We Pray for These and All," "Blowback"; *Poet Lore:* "In the Desert"; *Poetry* (Chicago): "Their Pleas"; *Seminary Ridge Review:* "Patterning"; *Southern Poetry Review:* "Everything

Lifted Off from the Earth"; *Southern Quarterly:* "Looking for My Dead Mother's Phone Number"; *Southern Review:* "This Universal Contraption"; *Sow's Ear:* "The World as Hologram"; *St. Katherine Review:* "Fantastic the Distances"; *Syzygy:* "Metaphor as Method," "Complicity," "Dark Energy," "Small Errors with Gigantic Consequences"; *The Northern Virginia Review:* "On Intuition"; *Vineyards:* "The Wind" and "The Visitors."

The following poems appeared in *Physics for Poets*, a chapbook published by Unicorn Press: "Alice These Days," "Alpha and Omega," "This Universal Contraption," "Musica Universalis," "Stars," "Fantastic the Distances," "SETI," "DNA," "Patterning," "Everything Lifted Off from the Earth," "On the Perception of Time," "Occam's Razor," "The God Particle," and "We Pray for These and All."

"The Right Words" was published by the Library of Virginia as a broadside for the Virginia Festival of the Book, 2012.

"A Dialogue between Mars and Venus" is reprinted from my collection *Relativity: A Point of View* (LSU, 1977).

"Of Love and Time" appeared in *Thirty-three,* ed. Sue Brannan Walker (Mobile, AL: Negative Capability Press, 2014). Rptd. in *Poetry Society of America Newsletter,* 2015.

www.ingramcontent.com/pod-product-compliance
Lightning Source LLC
Chambersburg PA
CBHW030122170426
43198CB00009B/701